LOVE & PASSION FOR THE ELDERLY

BY THE
SILVEY JEX PARTNERSHIP

Published in the UK by
POWERFRESH Limited
21 Rothersthorpe Crescent
Northampton
NN4 8JD

Telephone   0845 130 4565
Facsimile   0845 130 4563
E Mail   info@powerfresh.co.uk

Reprint 2003

ISBN 1 874125 961

Printed in the UK by Unwin Brothers Limited
Powerfresh April 2003

HELLO HANDSOME!

ARE YOU FOLLOWING ME YOUNG MAN?

SIGH! BY THE TIME WE'VE GOT OUR CLOTHES OFF, THE MOOD WILL HAVE GONE!

YES IT'S VERY NICE MR POTTER... NOW WHAT'S THIS ABOUT AN INGROWING TOE NAIL?

YOU'RE SUPPOSED TO GO TO SLEEP AFTER IT...NOT DURING IT!

YO SWEET SISTERS - EVERYTHING'S COOL . WHICH BABE'S GONNA
CHECK OUT WITH SUPER STUD AND GIT ON DOWN TO MY LOVE THANG!

I'VE LEFT MY TEETH SOMEWHERE...
YOU HAVEN'T SEEN THEM HAVE YOU JEFFERY?

I'M TINGLING WITH EXCITEMENT—OR IT COULD BE MY POOR CIRCULATION

IT'S ALRIGHT OLD GIRL ... I'M WEARING A CATHETER

IT'S LOVELY HERBERT — JUST WHAT I'VE ALWAYS WANTED

WHY CAN'T YOU SLEEP AFTER LUNCH LIKE <u>OTHER</u> OLD MEN?

...I HOPE YOU'RE READY FOR THIS MY DEAR...
I'VE GOT SOME JUMP LEADS ATTACHED TO THE YOUNG MAN NEXT DOOR

OH MR MARCO YOU SEXY BEAST—
LET'S GO BACK TO MY PLACE AFTER THE SHOW AND MAKE LOVE

TYING ME TO THE BED IS OKAY... BUT DID YOU <u>HAVE</u> TO USE A GRANNY KNOT?

FUNNY... WHEN I WAS YOUNG I ALWAYS FANCIED AN OLDER MAN...BUT NOW...

NO, NO-I SAID...I'VE GOT ACUTE <u>ANGINA</u> !!

AFTER YOU WITH THE TEETH, MY DARLING

STAY DOWN THERE MISS WILKINS, I THINK I HEAR MATRON COMING

...AND LOOK AT THE SHODDY CRAFTSMANSHIP ON THESE...
THEY'VE FORGOTTEN TO STITCH THE CROTCH UP.

DON'T LOOK DEAR.... THEY'LL ONLY GET SILLY

IF YOU'RE FREE... I'M FREE AND I MEAN <u>FREE</u>

I'D BETTER NOT GO DOWN....I WON'T BE ABLE TO GET UP AGAIN

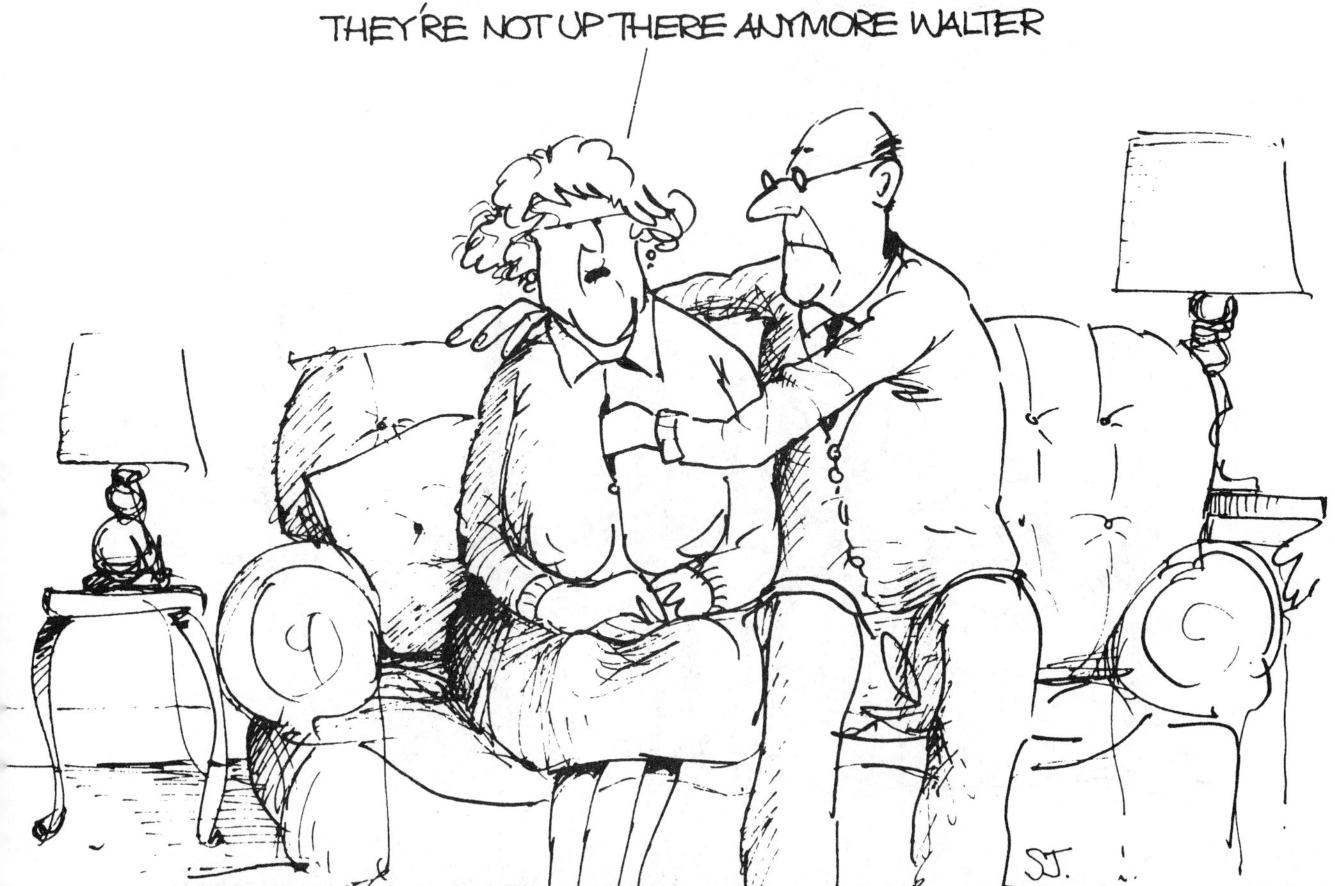
THEY'RE NOT UP THERE ANYMORE WALTER
SJ.

YOUR PERFUME IS DRIVING ME CRAZY... DEEP HEAT WAS ALWAYS MY FAVOURITE

ARE YOU GIRLS INTERESTED IN A GAME OF STRIP CRIBBAGE?

I SAID...OOH...AHH...YES..YES..OOH DON'T STOP...YES...YES..

PHEW! THESE RUBBER SHEETS GENERATE SOME HEAT DON'T THEY?

FOR GOD'S SAKE WOMAN GET OFF ME

WHAT WOULD YOU CHARGE FOR FIVE MINUTES LAP DANCING?

LOOK EVERYBODY—IT'S GEORGE BACK FROM HIS LITTLE TRANSPLANT OPERATION

WHAT DO YOU SAY WE POOL OUR PENSIONS AND GET A HOTEL ROOM?